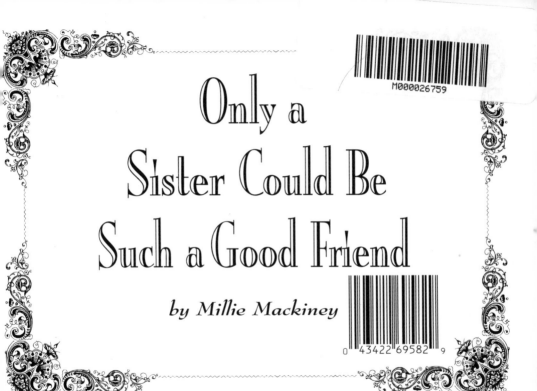

Only a
Sister Could Be
Such a Good Friend

by Millie Mackiney

Cover Design by MarketForce, Inc., Burr Ridge, IL
Typography by MarketForce, Inc.

Published by Great Quotations Publishing Co.,
Glendale Heights, IL

ISBN #1-56245-338-6

Library of Congress Catalog Number: 97-77654

Printed in Hong Kong.

Introduction

Writing this book allowed me a chance to glance back at the various relationships which have enriched my life. The common threads which weave through my memories are those I share with my sisters. This book celebrates this connection. I hope the quotes and passages I've selected give you occasion to appreciate this special union only you and your sisters could understand.

"Sisters"

"Sisters, sisters, there were never such devoted sisters. Never had to have a chaperone - No, Sir! I'm there to keep my eye on her.

4

"Sisters" 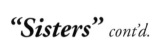 *cont'd.*

"Caring, sharing, every little
thing that we are wearing.
When a certain gentleman
arrived from Rome, she wore
the dress and I stayed home!

"Sisters" cont'd.

"All kinds of weather,
we stick together;
The same in the rain and sun.

"Sisters" *cont'd.*

"Two different faces,
but in tight places.
We think and we act as one.

7

"Sisters" cont'd.

"Those who've seen us, know that not a thing could come between us. Many men have tried to split us up, but no one can.

8

"*Sisters*" cont'd.

"Lord help the mister who comes between me and my sister. And Lord help the sister who comes between me and my man!"

by Irving Berlin

One's sister is a part of one's essential self, an eternal presence of one's heart and soul and memory.

— Susan Cahill

A sister is someone who...

Expects your best but
accepts your worst.

11

Both within the family
and without, our sisters hold
up our mirrors: our images
of who we are and who
we can dare to become.

— Elizabeth Fishel

12

She has three sisters...when they aggravate her, she wants to pinch their habits off like potato bugs off the leaf. But she meets them each weekend for cards and jokes, while months go by without her speaking to her brother.

— Minnie Bruce Pratt

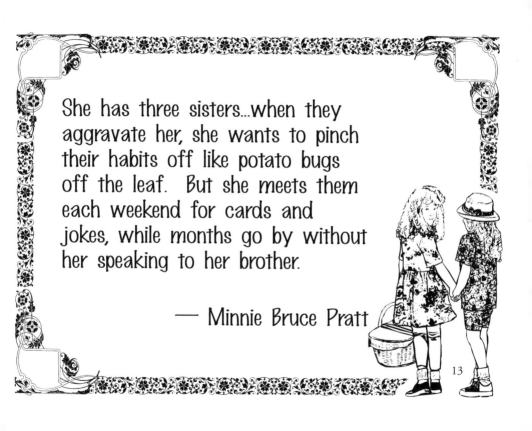

13

A sister listens to you complain about your husband but acts like she likes him anyway.

14

Sisters can be pets, or pet peeves.
A sister can be a friend, and a sister
can be a sister. However we may
regard them, either as our mirror
image or our opposites, sisters are
an important part of our lives.

— Lois L. Kaufman

The bond between women
is a circle – we are together
within it.

— Judy Grahn

16

When you fight with a brother or a sister, you're only hurting yourself, because they are a part of you.

— American Proverb

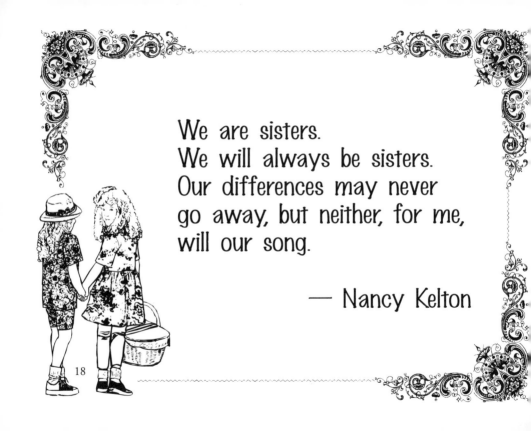

We are sisters.
We will always be sisters.
Our differences may never
go away, but neither, for me,
will our song.

— Nancy Kelton

18

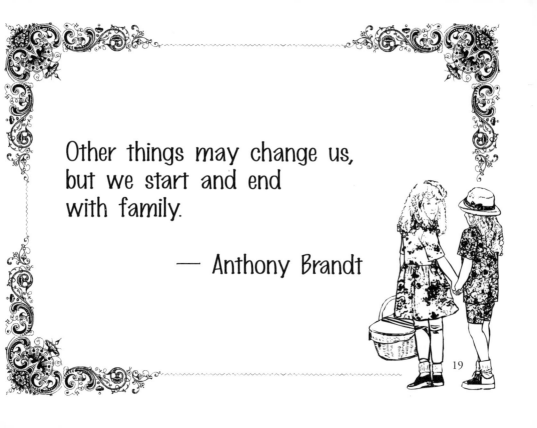

Other things may change us,
but we start and end
with family.

— Anthony Brandt

19

A sibling may be the sole keeper of one's core identity, the only person with the keys to one's unfettered, more fundamental self.

— Marian Sandmaier

20

A sister will tell you the truth when you're trying on clothes.

Of the many relationships in a woman's life, the bond between sisters is unique, stretching and bending through periods of closeness and distance, but almost never breaking.

— Carol Saline

A sister is your other self.

My sister never reminded
me of my self-righteousness
about child rearing before
I had my own.

— Elizabeth Rossignuolo

24

We acquire friends and
we make enemies, but our
sisters come with the territory.

— Evelyn Loeb

Children of the same mother
do not always agree.

— Nigerian Proverb

26

Sisters may share the same
mother and father, but
somehow appear to come
from entirely different families.

I sought my soul,
But my soul I could not see.
I sought my God,
But my God eluded me.
I sought my sisters,
and I found all three.

— Anon

28

Big sisters are the crabgrass
in the lawn of life.

— Charlie Brown.

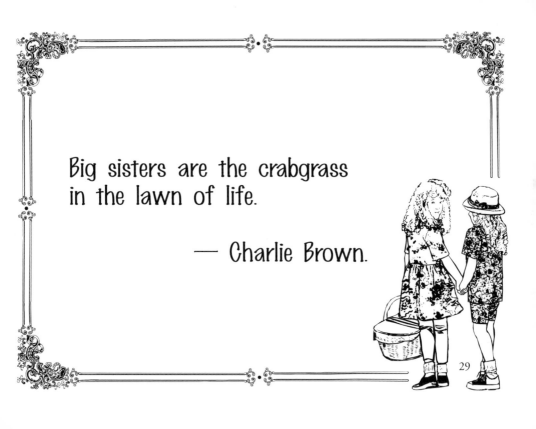

29

It is only the women
whose eyes have been
washed clear with tears who
get the broad vision that
makes them little sisters
to the world.

— Dorothy Dix

30

A sibling is any other kid
your mother and father have
around the house. You will
not like her. She will not like you.
Make friends with her anyway.
It evens up the odds with
your parents.

— R. P. Smith

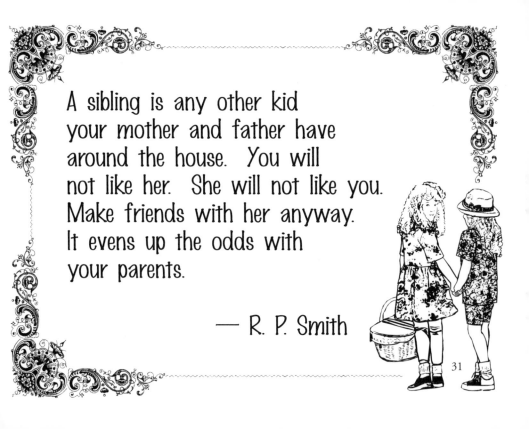

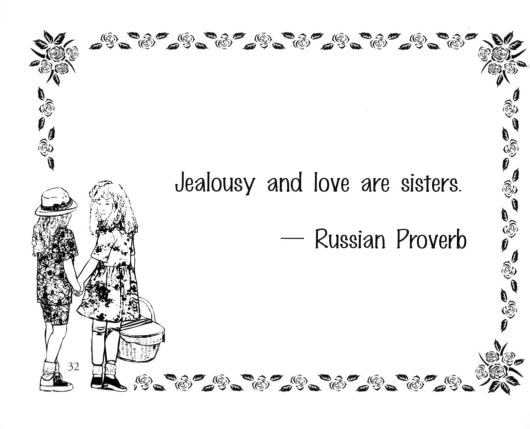

Jealousy and love are sisters.

— Russian Proverb

32

If you want to know
how old a woman is,
ask her sister-in-law.

— E. W. Howe

My sister is the friend who shows me what I want from other friends. She sets the standard everybody else has to match.

34

With patience, luck and the will to change, the quarrels of the early years fertilize the soil in which friendship takes root.

— Elizabeth Fishel

"How sister gazed at sister
reaching through mirrored
pupils back to the mother."

— Adrienne Rich

To have a loving relationship
with a sister is not simply
to have a buddy or a
confidant – it is to have
a soul mate for life.

— Victoria Secunda

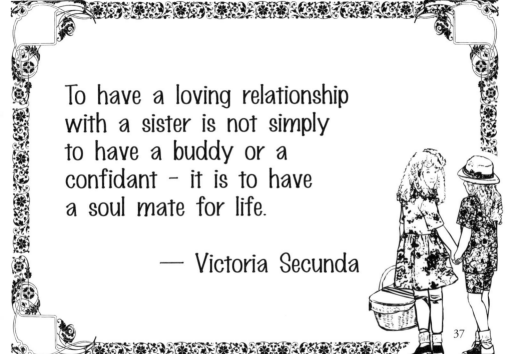

Together we look like
our mother. Her same eyes,
her same mouth, open in
surprise to see, at last,
her long-cherished wish.

— Amy Tan

38

You can't think how I
depend on you, and when
you're not there, the color
goes out of my life.

— Virginia Woolf

Friends grow up and
move away. Children come
and eventually they go.
But the one thing that's
never lost is your sister.

40

Sisters examine each other
so they can have a map
for how they should behave.

— Michael D. Kahn

For there is no friend like
a sister in calm or stormy
weather; To cheer one on the
tedious way, To fetch one if
one goes astray; To lift one if
one totters down; To strengthen
one whilst one stands.

— Christina Rosetti

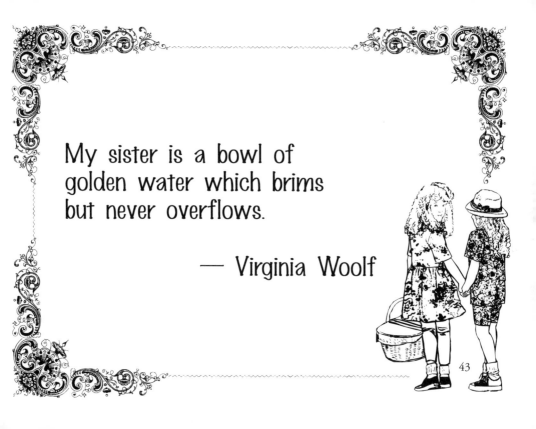

My sister is a bowl of
golden water which brims
but never overflows.

— Virginia Woolf

43

...a loving sister is an unconditional, narcissistic and complicated devotion that approximates a mother's love... sisters are inescapably connected, shaped by the same two parents, the same trove of memory and experience.

— Mary Bruno

44

The interweaving of these funny, joyful, angry, painful and historic childhood memories creates the foundation — solid or shaky — on which every sister relationship rests.

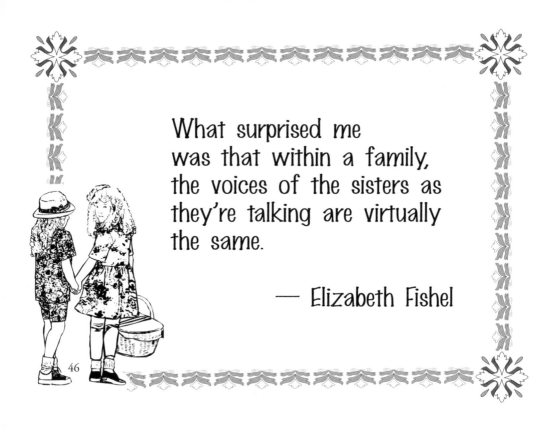

What surprised me
was that within a family,
the voices of the sisters as
they're talking are virtually
the same.

— Elizabeth Fishel

My grandmother told me
that friends may come
and go, but your sister
will always be there.

— Rachel Rossignuolo

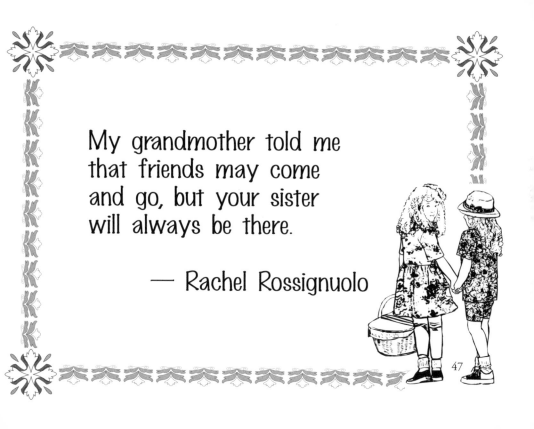

47

With sisters, the joy
is multiplied and the
grief divided.

48

A sister can be a counselor,
a listener, a spiritual teacher,
not a preacher, a helper,
a doer, a friend who can't
be any truer.

— Janice Weatherall Clark

Any mother who can keep peace in a family of sisters could run the world.

The young ladies entered
the drawing room in the full
fervor of sisterly animosity.

— R. S. Surtees

51

Blest pair of sirens,
pledges of heaven's joy,
Sphere born harmonious
sisters, voice and verse.

— John Milton

52

It is a great comfort to have
an artistic sister.

— Louisa May Alcott

I have a brother who wants to be President, one sister who rides motorcycles and another who is a holy roller preacher. That makes me the only sane one in the family.

— Billy Carter (1978)

Comparison is a death knell
to sisterly harmony.

Never praise a sister to a sister, in the hope of your compliments reaching the proper ears.

— Rudyard Kipling

56

Sisters, whatever their stories, instinctively know how fortunate they are.

— Susan Ripps

Sisterhood: a rich, evocative celebration of an unbreakable bond.

58

Imps and angels simultaneously,
they hover on the sidelines of all
the other choices and connections
– spouses, professions, children,
friendships – that we make,
sometimes lending a hand or ear
but often simply taken for granted.

— Susan Scarf Merrell

There's a certain intimacy that makes them so different from close friends. Sisterhood is such a powerful relationship.

— Carol Saline

60

My sister:

She knows how you've changed,
how you've grown through the years,
and she knows all that you're
dreaming of, she's the comfort of
family, the warm touch of home...
She's a beautiful blessing of love.

— Amanda Bradley

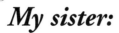

A sister is a part of yourself that responds to you. You can see it and feel it. This person you grew up with and shared everything with, who has your genes and your blood and is so much like you, yet also different. You can't get the same thing from friends.

Sisterly love is, of all
sentiments, the most abstract.
Nature does not give it
any functions.

— Ugo Betti

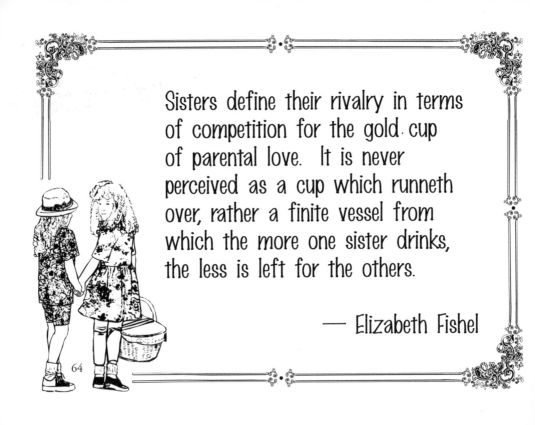

Sisters define their rivalry in terms of competition for the gold cup of parental love. It is never perceived as a cup which runneth over, rather a finite vessel from which the more one sister drinks, the less is left for the others.

— Elizabeth Fishel

64

A ministering angel
shall my sister be.

— William Shakespeare

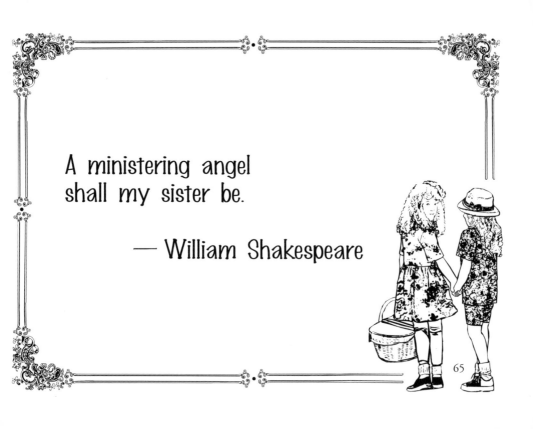

Sisterhood among women
in general has never been
so significant as at present.
It is a growing movement,
and promises to change
the course of our history.

— Lois L. Kaufman

66

A sister will swap kids,
clothes and books.

There are women who don't have a good relationship with their sisters but who wish it were otherwise. Having kids can be a turning point. Their relationship can become revitalized and reinvigorated.

— Michael Kahn

To my sister —

You can't think how I depend
on you, and when you're
not there, the colour goes
out of my life.

— Virginia Woolf

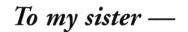

First an acquaintance, then a friend. Shared your hopes, thoughts, dreams and fears: Now you have a sister til the end.

— Janice Weatherall Clark

70

Of the constants that rest
in the heart, a sister's a primary part.
She'll always be there when you
need her–you listen, you value, you
heed her. As growth, independence
you ponder, your feelings grow
deeper and fonder; and life tells you
one thing that's true: A sister's
a large part of you.

— Bruce B. Wilmer

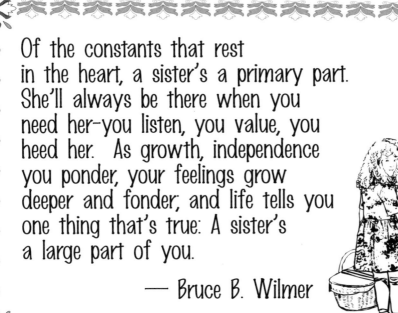

A sister will lend you her kids when Disney has a new movie that you want to see, and all your kids are in college.

72

She shared much with her
sister — they had one bike
and one sled between them
and had learned long ago
that these possessions were
not worth the fights.

— Ann McGovern

73

My Sister —

She's a friend who brings sunshine
and laughter your way. She
supported you in all that you do.
She's been at the heart of so
many glad moments and shares
precious moments with you...

— Amanda Bradley

The older daughter is married off by her parents, the younger daughter by her sister.

— Russian Proverb

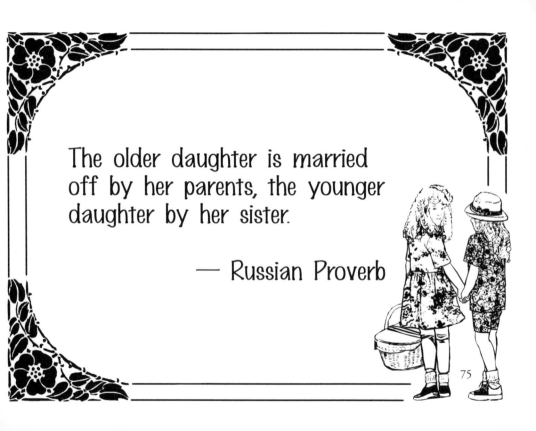

A sister is both your mirror —
and your opposite.

— Elizabeth Fishel

76

Sometimes I still feel the same way I did when Mother brought you home from the hospital — "I don't want it, take it back."

A sister is a lifelong friend.

78

No one knows better than
a sister how we grew up,
and who our friends,
teachers and favorite toys
were. No one knows better
than she.

— Dale V. Atkins

I cannot say that now I am without your company. I feel not only that I am deprived of a very dear sister, but that I have lost half of myself.

— Beatrice D'Este

Sisters examine each other
so they can have a map
for how they should behave.

— Michael D. Kahn

We are each other's reference point at our turning points.

— Elizabeth Fishel

Sisters —

Often, in old age, they become
each other's chosen and most happy
companions. In addition to their shared
memories of childhood and of their
relationship to each other's children,
they share memories of the same home.

— Margaret Mead

83

An older sister helps one
remain half child, half woman.

84

Sisterhood is the journey
of sharing each other's
happiness and comforting
each other's tears.

No people are ever as divided
as those of the same blood.

— Mavis Gallant

What sets sisters apart
from brothers and also from
friends is a very intimate
meshing of heart, soul and
the mystical cords of memory.

— Carol Saline

It doesn't matter whether or not we had similar interests or lifestyles. We learned to love each other as children, and we never stopped.

To have a loving relationship
with a sister is not simply to
have a buddy or confidante;
it is to have a soul mate
for life.

— Victoria Secunda

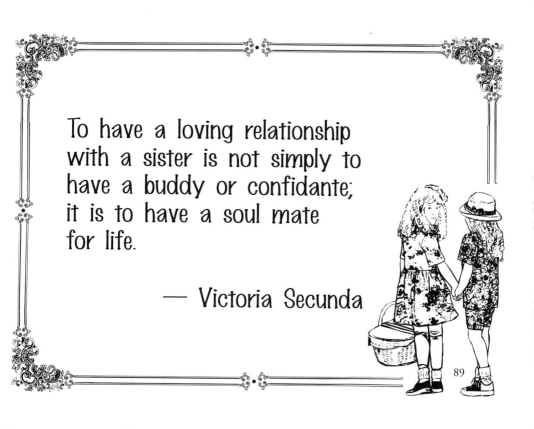

Sisters probably have the most competitive relationship within the family, but once the sisters are grown, it becomes the strongest relationship.

— Margaret Mead

90

It is not so much our sisters'
help that helps us as the
confident knowledge that
they will help us.

— Epicurus

Silence can make a
conversation between sisters.
It's the not needing to say
anything that really counts.

I am not afraid to trust
my sisters.

— Angelina Grimke

Each person grows not only by her own talents and development of her inner beliefs, but also by what she receives from the persons around her.

— Iris Haberli

94

My sister —

You give me a solid
foundation and a sense of
when I stray too far from
the norm. I know that
I have a best friend for my
entire life who is never
going to go away.

Sisters function as safety nets in a chaotic world simply by being there for each other.

— Carol Saline

96

A constant friend is a thing
rare and hard to find.

— Plutarch

97

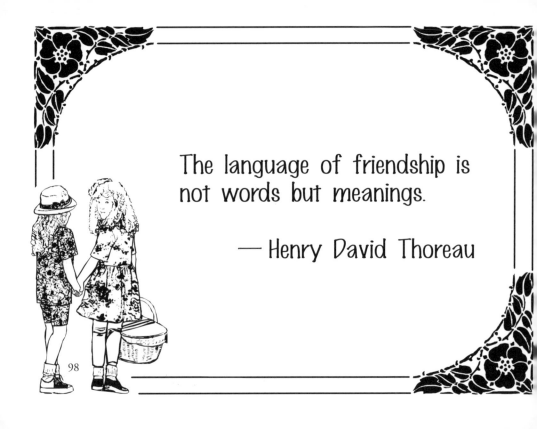

The language of friendship is not words but meanings.

— Henry David Thoreau

98

If I can stop one heart from breaking, I shall not live in vain; If I can ease one life the aching, or cool one pain, or help one fainting robin unto his nest again, I shall not live in vain.

— Emily Dickinson

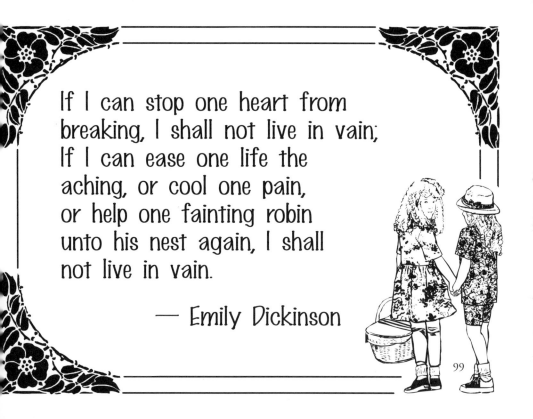

I don't expect the same things from my brothers that I do my sisters.
I expect my brothers to be there when I need them, but I expect my sisters to finish my sentences for me and always know what I mean no matter how badly I may say it.
Sisters stand between one and life's cruel circumstances.

— Nancy Mitford

100

A sister is someone who turns the light on to show you there's nothing to be afraid of in the dark.

There is no outsider anywhere who wouldn't appreciate and even envy the tremendous advantage that sisters have, if properly utilized, against all odds.

— Susan Ripps

102

I recognize how crucial my
relationship with my sister is
in the definition of myself.

— Barbara Mathias

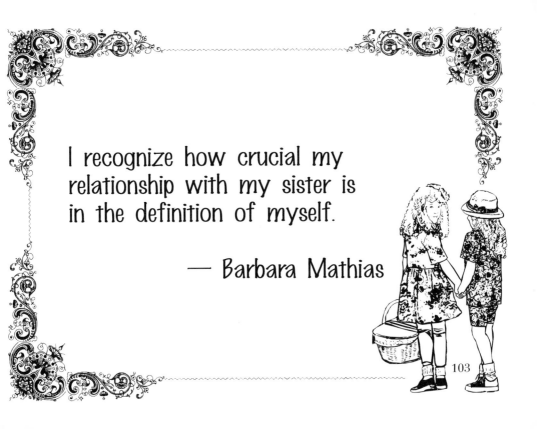

A sister knows what you're really thinking, especially when you can't say it.

Women have a way of
treating people more softly.
We treat souls with kid gloves.

— Shirley Ceaser

We are together, my mother
and I. Mother and child,
yes, but sisters really,
against whatever denies us
all that we are.

— Alice Walker

106

Having a sister means having one of the most beautiful and unique of human relationships. We share with our sisters a special intimacy, a communion of heart and mind more powerful than any friendship.

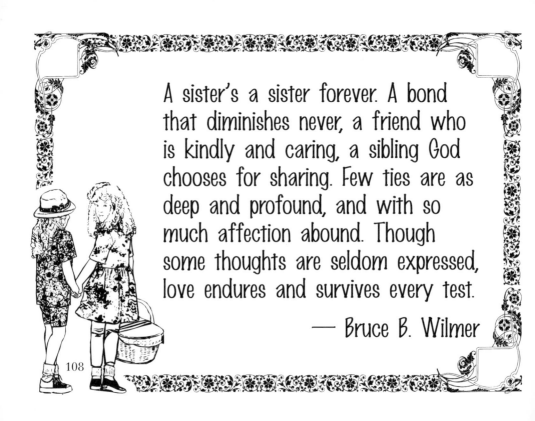

A sister's a sister forever. A bond that diminishes never, a friend who is kindly and caring, a sibling God chooses for sharing. Few ties are as deep and profound, and with so much affection abound. Though some thoughts are seldom expressed, love endures and survives every test.

— Bruce B. Wilmer

108

The desire to be and have a sister is a primitive and profound one that may have everything or nothing to do with the family a woman is born to. It is a desire to know and be known by someone who shares blood, history, dreams, common ground and the unknown adventures of the future.

— Elizabeth Fishel

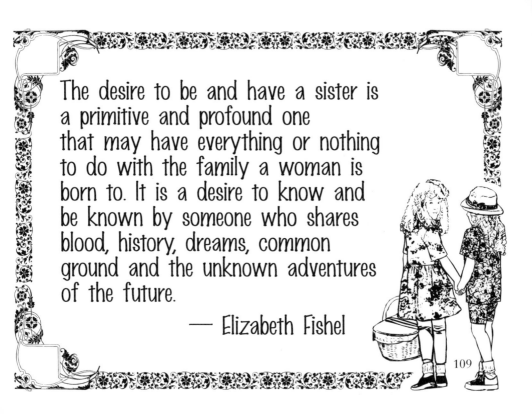

109

Being a good friend, and having a good friend, can enrich your days and bring you lifelong satisfaction. But friendships don't just happen. They have to be created and nurtured. Like any other skill, building friendship has to be practiced.

— Sue Browder

110

Sensitive to your needs.

Inspires you to keep "hangin' in there".

Share their most intimate secrets with you.

There to tell you about all those "first times"

Encourage you when no one else will.

Remind you of all those things you'd rather forget.

Shelter you from harm, hurt or pain.

— Janice Weatherall-Clark

There is nothing I could do,
no disagreement I could have that
would make my sister not love me.
We belong to each other and that
is inviolate. We contribute to the
solidarity of our bond by being there
when we're needed - by carrying our
own weight. You don't mess with
that kind of stuff. You invest in it.

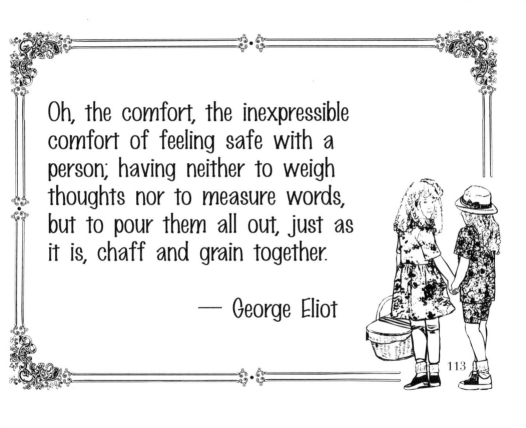

Oh, the comfort, the inexpressible comfort of feeling safe with a person; having neither to weigh thoughts nor to measure words, but to pour them all out, just as it is, chaff and grain together.

— George Eliot

113

That is the best — to laugh
with someone because you
both think the same things
are funny.

— Gloria Vanderbilt

114

Thought fitted thought;
opinion met opinion:
we coincided, in short, perfectly.

— Charlotte Brontë

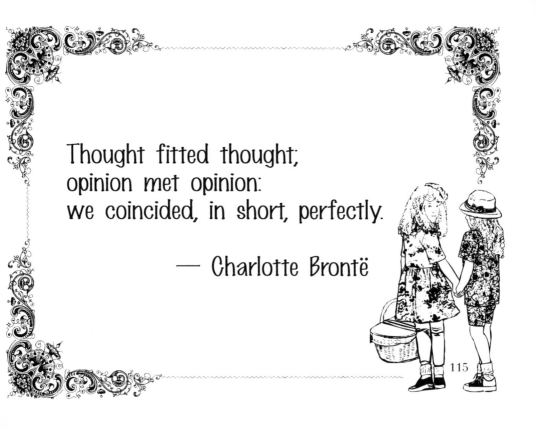

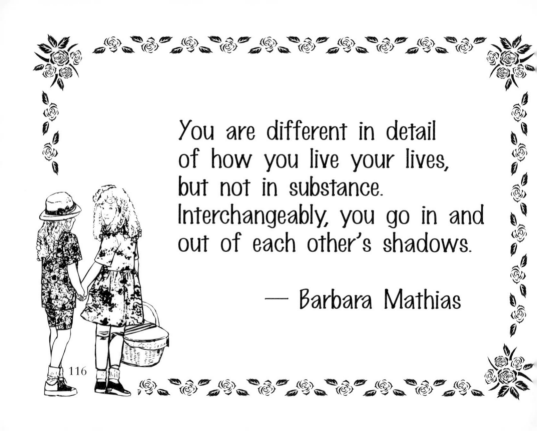

You are different in detail
of how you live your lives,
but not in substance.
Interchangeably, you go in and
out of each other's shadows.

— Barbara Mathias

A sister never tires of talking
on the phone about nothing.

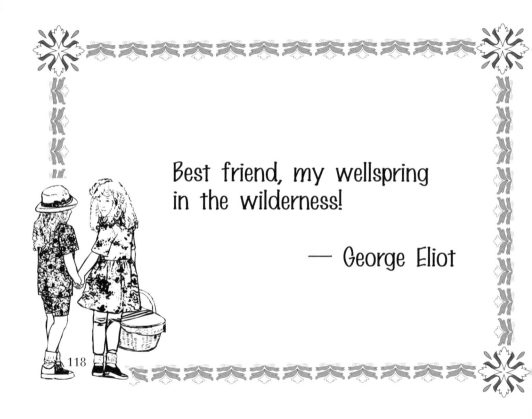

Best friend, my wellspring
in the wilderness!

— George Eliot

118

Our brothers and sisters are there with us from the dawn of our personal stories to the inevitable dusk.

— Susan Scarf Merrill

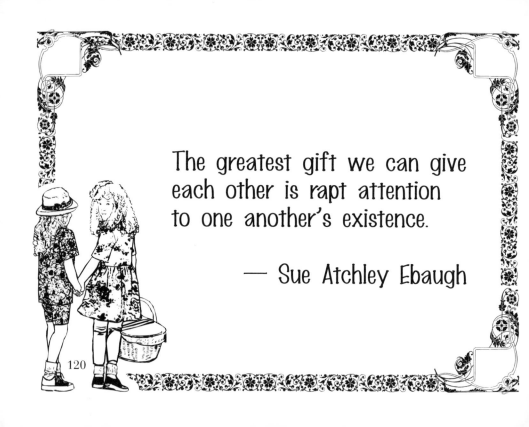

The greatest gift we can give
each other is rapt attention
to one another's existence.

— Sue Atchley Ebaugh

120

Hold a true friend with both your hands.

— Nigerian Proverb

In thee my soul shall own combined (sic) the sister and the friend.

— Catherine Killigrew

122

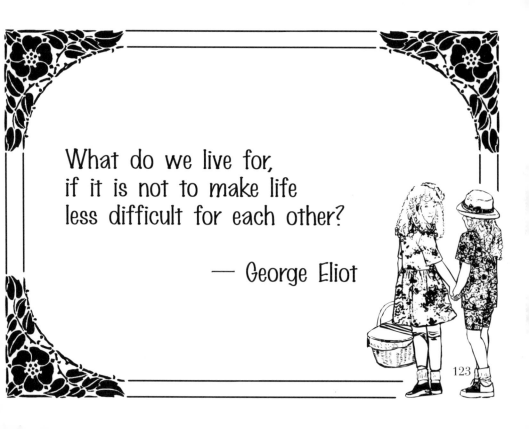

What do we live for,
if it is not to make life
less difficult for each other?

— George Eliot

123

A sister is someone you can call at 3 a.m. and know she won't hang up on you.

124

Alone we can do so little,
together we can do so much.

— Helen Keller

A sister speaks the language
of your heart.

If you have one true friend,
you have more than your
share comes to.

— Thomas Fuller

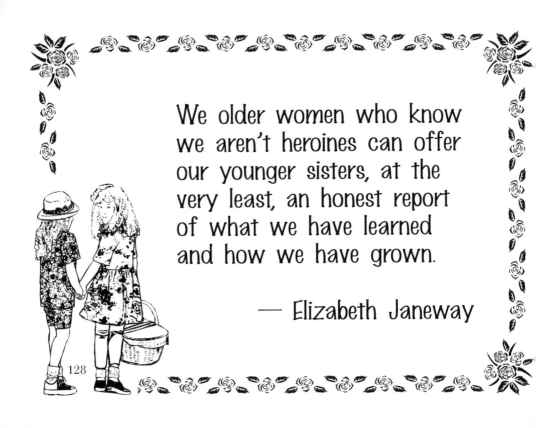

We older women who know
we aren't heroines can offer
our younger sisters, at the
very least, an honest report
of what we have learned
and how we have grown.

— Elizabeth Janeway

I didn't belong as a kid, and
that always bothered me.
If only I'd known that one day
my differentness would be
an asset, then my early life
would have been much easier.

— Bette Midler

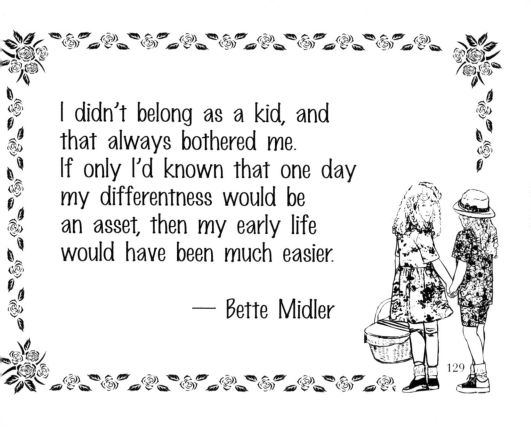

No matter how many
communes anybody invents,
the family always creeps back.

— Margaret Mead

130

When you look at your life,
the greatest happinesses are
family happinesses.

— Dr. Joyce Brothers

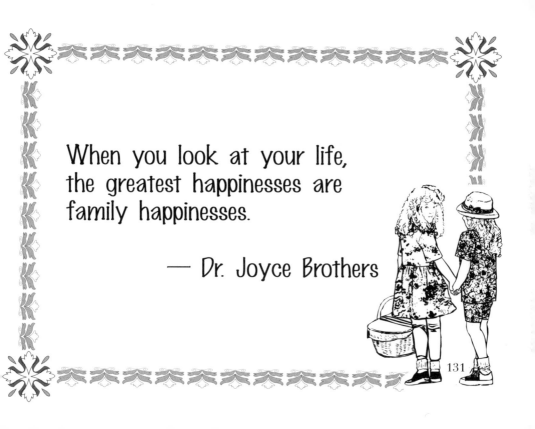

The older I get, the simpler
my fantasies. Two women
sitting across a table from
each other, two cups of
coffee, strong as the love.

— Pam Houston

132

Family jokes, though rightly cursed by strangers, are the bond that keeps most families alive.

— Stella Benson

Writing this, I realize how sweet and slippery is this word "sister" – big enough to stretch beyond biology and across time; flexible enough to define soulmates and virtual strangers.

— Letty Cottin Pogrebin

134

My sister! With that thrilling word Let thoughts unnumbered wildly spring! What echoes in my heart are stirred, While thus I touch the trembling string.

— Margaret Davidson

As the standard bearers of our first families, our siblings are the only people who can truly share our happy and unhappy memories with us, who can help reconstruct that early sense that the world was manageable and we would always be cared for.

— Susan Scarf Merrell

136

Home is not where you live but where they understand you.

— Christian Morgenstern

A home-made friend wears longer than one you buy in the market.

— Austin O'Malley

138

Sons branch out, but one
woman leads to another.

— Margaret Atwood

Childhood is the kingdom where nobody dies.

— Edna St. Vincent Millay

140

Family faces are
magic mirrors. Looking at
people who belong to us,
we see the past, present
and future.

— Gail Lumet Buckley

Call it a clan, call it a network, call it a tribe, call it a family. Whatever you call it, whomever you are, you need one.

— Jane Howard

What families have in common the world around is that they are the place where people learn who they are and how to be that way.

— Jean Illsley Clarke

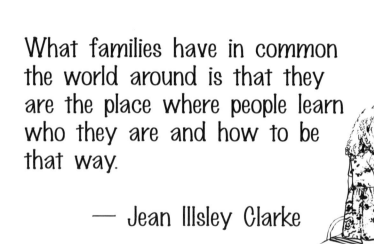

143

Our siblings – they resemble us just enough to make all their differences confusing, and no matter what we choose to make of this, we are cast in relation to them our whole lives long.

— Susan Scarf Merrell

To the family – the dear
octopus from whose tentacles
we never quite escape, nor,
in our inmost hearts,
ever quite wish to.

— Dodie Smith

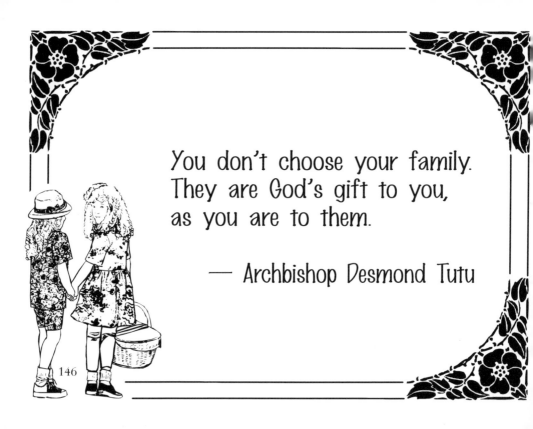

You don't choose your family.
They are God's gift to you,
as you are to them.

— Archbishop Desmond Tutu

146

Sisterhood – that is, primary
and bonding love from women –
is, like motherhood, a capacity,
not a destiny. It must be chosen,
exercised by acts of will.

— Olga Broumas

To look at one's sister is to look at the other and realize that even with the most unflinching scrutiny, all bets are off. To know a sister is to know paradox.

— Patricia Foster

Sometimes, sisters have the same journey in their hearts. One may help the other or betray her. Will they cross over? Will the ship sail without them?

— Louise Bernikow

The pull between sisters is the realization of similarity versus the need for difference.

— Elizabeth Fishel

150

Jamie (Lee) and I have run
the gamut, from tearing each
other's hair out when we
were kids, to ignoring each
other, to becoming each
other's best friend.

— Kelly Curtis

I don't believe that the accident of birth makes people sisters or brothers. It makes them siblings. Gives them mutuality of parentage. Sisterhood and brotherhood is a condition people have to work at.

— Maya Angelou

Family is just accident...
they don't mean to get on
your nerves. They don't even
mean to be your family,
they just are.

— Marsha Norman

153

Fond as we are of our loved ones, there comes at times during their absence, an unexplained peace.

— Anne Shaw

154

There is space within
sisterhood for likeness and
difference, for the subtle
differences that challenge
and delight; there is space
for disappointment —
and surprise.

— Christine Downing

155

You can't give up a sister.
You were born with them,
and you die with them.

— Elizabeth Mead Steig

156

All things evolve and are
involved in a pattern of
struggle and release.
This includes sisterhood.

— Joy Harjo

We share space in the family with them, we learn from them and teach them, we divide up parental loyalties with them, we envy them, admire them, dominate them, hate them, love them.

— Susan Scarf Merrell

158

Lying in the cradle was my dearest friend and bitterest rival, my mirror and opposite, my confidante and betrayer, my student and teacher...my subordinate, my superior and, scarier still, my equal.

— Elizabeth Fishel

Sibling rivalry is not an evil
born of parental failure.
It is a fact of life.

— Seymour V. Reit

160

A sister remembers the
"good old days" with you,
even if they weren't.

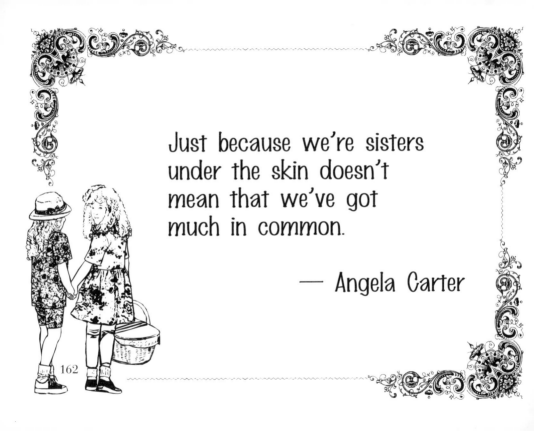

Just because we're sisters
under the skin doesn't
mean that we've got
much in common.

— Angela Carter

162

The relationship between two siblings is perhaps more like a cactus than an oak, for it requires less watering than other friendships to survive.

— Susan Scarf Merrell

163

Love involves a peculiar,
unfathomable combination
of understanding and
misunderstanding.

— Diane Arbus

164

From the psychological
jousting between sisters
in the early family arena
emerge the first tentative
boundaries of their personalities.

— Elizabeth Fishel

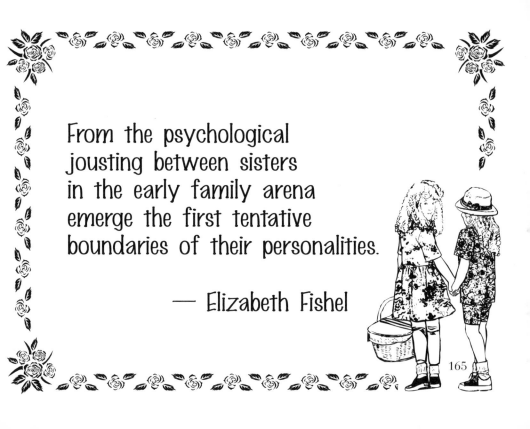

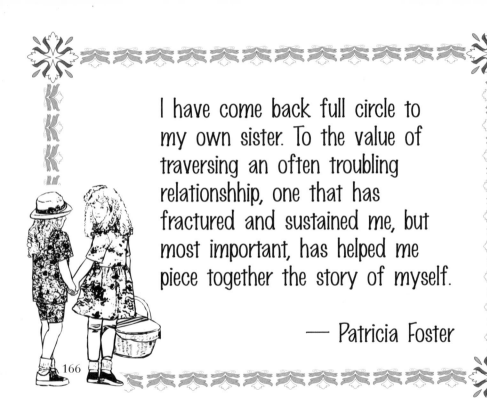

I have come back full circle to my own sister. To the value of traversing an often troubling relationshhip, one that has fractured and sustained me, but most important, has helped me piece together the story of myself.

— Patricia Foster

A sister can be seen as someone who is both ourselves and very much not ourselves – a special kind of double.

— Toni Morrison

Other Titles by Great Quotations

301 Ways to Stay Young At Heart
The ABC's of Parenting
African-American Wisdom
Angel-grams
As A Cat Thinketh
Astrology for Cats
Astrology for Dogs
The Be-Attitudes
The Birthday Astrologer
Can We Talk
Celebrating Women
Chicken Soup
Chocoholic Reasonettes
The Cornerstones of Success
Daddy & Me
Erasing My Sanity
Fantastic Father, Dependable Dad
Golden Years, Golden Words
Graduation Is Just The Beginning
Grandma, I Love You
Happiness is Found Along The Way
High Anxieties
Hooked on Golf

I Didn't Do It
I'm Not Over the Hill
Ignorance is Bliss
Inspirations
Interior Design for Idiots
The Lemonade Handbook
Let's Talk Decorating
Life's Lessons
Life's Simple Pleasures
A Lifetime of Love
A Light Heart Lives Long
Looking for Mr. Right
Midwest Wisdom
Mommy & Me
Mother, I Love You
The Mother Load
Motivating Quotes
    for Motivated People
Mrs. Murphy's Laws
Mrs. Webster's Dictionary
My Daughter, My Special Friend
Only a Sister
The Other Species

Parenting 101
Pink Power
Reflections
Romantic Rhapsody
The Secret Language of Men
The Secret Language of Women
The Secrets in Your Face
The Secrets in Your Name
A Servant's Heart
Social Disgraces
Some Things Never Change
The Sports Page
Sports Widow
Stress or Sanity
A Teacher is Better Than
    Two Books
TeenAge of Insanity
Thanks from the Heart
Things You'll Learn...
A Touch of Friendship
Wedding Wonders
Words From The Coach
Working Woman's World

Great Quotations, Publishing Company

1967 Quincy Court
Glendale Heights, IL 60139 USA
Phone: 630-582-2800   Fax: 630-582-2813
http://www.greatquotations.com